T0012205

The
SMALL and MIGHTY
Book of
Deadly
Creatures

Published in 2023 by OHI.
An imprint of Welbeck Children's Limited, part of Welbeck Publishing Group
Offices in: London – 20 Mortimer Street, London W1T 3JW
and Sydney – 205 Commonwealth Street, Surry Hills 2010
www.welbeckpublishing.com

A CIP catalogue record for this book is available from the British Library.

Writer: Clive Gifford
Illustrator: Isabel Muñoz
Consultant: Paul Lawston
Design and editorial by Raspberry Books Ltd
Editorial Manager: Tash Mosheim
Design Manager: Russell Porter
Production: Jess Brisley

ISBN 978 1 80069 461 3

Printed in Heshan, China

10 9 8 7 6 5 4 3 2 1

FSC
www.fsc.org
MIX
Paper | Supporting
responsible forestry
FSC® C020056

The
SMALL and MIGHTY
Book of
Deadly
Creatures

Clive Gifford and Isabel Muñoz

Contents

INTRODUCTION

〜

This little book is absolutely bursting
with facts about some of the deadliest
creatures on planet Earth.

Dangerous animals come in all shapes
and sizes, from tiny insects to powerful
polar bears and sperm whales
bigger than a school bus. Some have
terrifying teeth or killer claws, while
others rely on speed, a powerful bite,
or deadly venom.

In this book you will find . . .

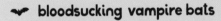
- bloodsucking vampire bats
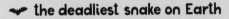
- the deadliest snake on Earth
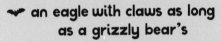
- an eagle with claws as long as a grizzly bear's
- the creature that's the most dangerous for people

. . . and lots more.

Read on to find out fascinating facts about these amazing animals.

Deadly on Land

Between 81,000
and 138,000 people die
EACH YEAR from
SNAKE BITES.

∽

THE MOST DEADLY SNAKES ARE:

1. Saw-scaled viper
2. Indian cobra
3. Common krait
4. Russell's viper

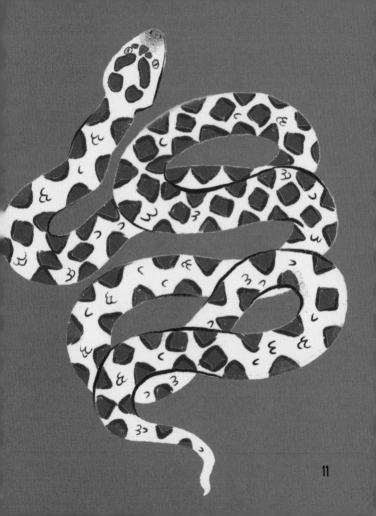

∽ THE ∽
FLIGHTLESS CASSOWARY
is a shy bird from Australia.
but if threatened. it can be deadly.

It weighs up to 175 lb., and can give a powerful kick
with its large, curved claws. The outermost claw
on each foot is the most dangerous:
it can tear terrible wounds that could
easily kill a human being.

THE GABOON VIPER is a large venomous snake that uses its FANGED TEETH to inject VENOM into its prey.

The viper's fangs can be 2 in. long—the biggest among venomous snakes.

They fold up flat so that they can fit inside the snake's mouth!

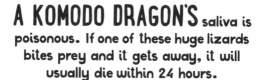

A KOMODO DRAGON'S saliva is
poisonous. If one of these huge lizards
bites prey and it gets away, it will
usually die within 24 hours.

Komodo dragons can eat as much as
four-fifths of their own body weight
in a single meal.

14

The **FIRE SALAMANDER** uses its **powerful poison** for defense. When threatened, it lowers its head and **sprays an attacker** with a cloud of poison from glands found above its eyes.

Fire salamanders can **break off their toes**, tails, and legs to get away if a predator grabs them. **Then they grow new ones!**

The VENOM from a **BLACK MAMBA'S** bite is very strong. Just two drops is enough to **KILL** an adult human.

16

A **SPITTING COBRA** ATTACKS PREY WITH ITS VENOM-FILLED FANGS. IT CAN ALSO DEFEND ITSELF FROM ATTACK BY SQUIRTING VENOM UP TO 10 FT. FORWARD, AIMING AT THE EYES OF ITS ATTACKER.

FOUND ONLY IN MADAGASCAR, THE **FOSSA** IS THE SIZE OF A COUGAR BUT IS RELATED TO MONGOOSES.

Sometimes one fossa will climb a tree and chase a creature down to the ground, where another fossa is waiting to **pounce**.

A CHEETAH'S
SPEED MAKES
IT DEADLY
TO OTHER
ANIMALS ON
THE AFRICAN
PLAINS.

CHEETAHS HUNT SMALL
TO MEDIUM-SIZED ANIMALS,
INCLUDING ANTELOPES AND
HARES, AND SOMETIMES TEAM
UP WITH OTHER CHEETAHS
TO HUNT BIGGER PREY, SUCH
AS WILDEBEESTS.

A LEOPARD

can leap up to 20 ft.,
and its top sprinting speed
is 36 mph—far faster
than you can run!

Leopards don't tend to attack people,

but they do hunt a wider range of prey than any other big cat, eating anything from DUNG BEETLES and FISH to ANTELOPES, MONKEYS, and DEER.

～

Leopards will sometimes carry their prey up to the high branches of a tree so that they can eat in peace, away from hyenas and other scavengers on the ground.

THE INLAND TAIPAN SNAKE, WHICH LIVES IN PARTS OF AUSTRALIA, HAS A PARTICULARLY STRONG VENOM. A BITE FROM THIS SNAKE CONTAINS ENOUGH **VENOM** TO KILL OVER 100 PEOPLE!

CONSTRICTORS are snakes that don't bite their prey. Instead, they wrap their muscly body around their victim tightly, squeeze, and stop its blood from flowing.

~ LIONESSES ~

do almost all of the hunting in a pride of lions. Only one in four lion hunts is successful.

In 1898, railroad builders in Kenya were **terrorized** by a pair of **Tsavo lions.** The lions are thought to have killed at least **35** people and perhaps many more.

When a river is full of
SALMON, a **GRIZZLY BEAR**
can catch and eat 30 fish
a day. Grizzlies sometimes
HUNT and **EAT**
OTHER BEARS.

GRIZZLY BEARS
CAN ALSO BE DEADLY TO
MOTHS! SOME GRIZZLIES IN
THE WESTERN UNITED STATES
EAT UP TO **40,000**
ARMY CUTWORM MOTHS
A DAY.

~ A GOLDEN ~ POISON DART FROG

measures less than 2.5 in. long and weighs just around 1 oz.—about the weight of five or six grapes.

Yet the small amount of **DEADLY POISON** on its skin is enough to kill up to ten people!

~

Tigers are great
nighttime hunters.
Their night vision is **six times**
better than ours, and they have soft
pads on their paws so that they can
prowl silently as they hunt.

32

TIGERS mostly hunt deer but also wild pigs, buffaloes, and even porcupines, despite their sharp quills. One large deer can feed a tiger for a week.

~

A tiger known as the Champawat Tigress was said to have killed 400 people in India and Nepal during an eight-year killing spree in the late 1800s and early 1900s.

There are fewer than 4,000 tigers left in the wild, but at least 5,000 are kept in zoos, parks and as pets in the United States.

HIPPOPOTAMUSES eat a plant-based diet, but they can be formidable attackers with their sharp tusks, bulky bodies, and giant mouths. They kill up to 500 people in Africa each year.

~

JAGUARS

roam up to 6 mi. a night in
search of food. They will kill animals
bigger than themselves with a
powerful bite to the back
of the neck.

When unfurled,
a chameleon's **TONGUE** can be
two and a half times the length of
its body. The creature **FLICKS** its
tongue out to catch crickets and other
insects at **LIGHTNING-FAST
SPEEDS.**

THE ROSETTE-NOSED CHAMELEON'S
TONGUE GOES FROM ZERO TO 60 MPH
IN JUST ONE-HUNDREDTH
OF A SECOND!

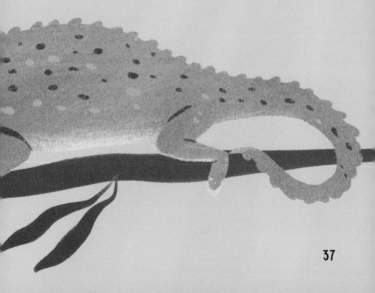

The **perentie** is Australia's **largest lizard.** It can swing its **powerful** tail with great force to **break** another creature's leg bones. It also has a **venomous** bite.

Perenties can grow up to around
8 ft. long and have been known to
eat **young kangaroos**, birds, and
even smaller members of their own species.

39

LIONS can sprint short distances at up to 50 mph.

Their ROAR can be heard more than 5 mi. away.

A male lion can eat up to 90 lb. of meat in a single sitting—that's more than 350 quarter-pound hamburgers!

Small but
Deadly

Many **MILLIONS** of **ARMY ANTS** can form a column that hunts together across a rainforest floor.

A column can kill **100,000** creatures—mostly insects but also sometimes FROGS, LIZARDS, and small MAMMALS that don't get out of the ants' path!

FOUR KINDS OF ANTS THAT ARE DANGEROUS TO PEOPLE:

~

1. Bulldog ant (also known as bull ants, the most dangerous to people—they can kill in 15 minutes)

2. Bullet ant (thought to have the most painful bite)

3. Fire ants

4. Red harvester ant

army ant

~ THE BRAZILIAN ~
WANDERING SPIDER

from South America
contains enough VENOM
to KILL an adult human
being. It's sometimes
found in bunches
of bananas!

There are some 7,000 species of **ASSASSIN BUGS**. Most **inject powerful saliva** into their victims, which include animals such as bees. The saliva **DISSOLVES THE PREY** from the inside, then the assassin bug **SLURPS** it up like soup.

MOSQUITOES

spread malaria as well as other diseases that are deadly to people, including dengue fever and yellow fever.

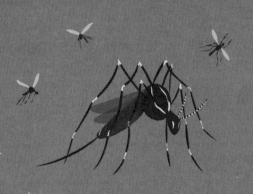

Only female
mosquitoes bite. They
puncture the skin with
a needle-like mouthpart
and then suck out a tiny
amount of blood.

Some species of female mosquitoes are
particularly attracted to sweaty,
smelly human feet!

The **TRAPDOOR SPIDER** is quite an **ENGINEER**.

IT BUILDS A BURROW COVERED BY A HINGED DOOR AND TRIP WIRES MADE OF ITS SILK.

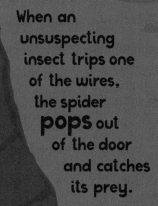

When an unsuspecting insect trips one of the wires, the spider **POPS** out of the door and catches its prey.

50

A trapdoor spider's DIET can include FROGS, baby SNAKES, and small rodents such as MICE.

The yellow-legged GIANT centipede BITES

victims with its tiny fangs, which inject a small amount of venom into its prey and can kill a mouse in 30 seconds.

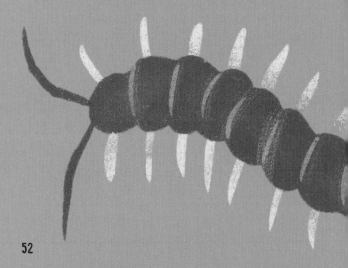

It can also be dangerous to people.

54

A DRAGONFLY'S EYE CONTAINS AS MANY AS **20,000** TINY COMPOUND LENSES. THESE GIVE IT INCREDIBLE EYESIGHT SO THAT IT CAN TRACK FAST-MOVING INSECT PREY THROUGH THE AIR.

~

Dragonfly young, called nymphs, live underwater. They are also ferocious predators and eat worms, tadpoles, small insects, and fish. They can shoot out their lower jaw, which is filled with sharp teeth, to capture their prey.

The 2 in. long caterpillar of the

GIANT SILKWORM MOTH

is considered the world's

DEADLIEST

caterpillar. It's covered in
hundreds of little spines, each coated
with a powerful venom.

More than 500 people
are thought to have died
because of these little
creatures.

A small cloud
of **poison gas** can be emitted
by the *Apheloria* millipede.
The gas contains enough **poison** to
kill small birds or mice.

THE
GOLIATH BIRD-EATING
SPIDER

only occasionally eats birds, but it also
eats mice, frogs, and large cockroaches.
With a body length of 5 in. and a 12 in.
leg span (which would cover a dinner plate),
it is one of the world's biggest spiders.

**DESPITE THE SPIDER'S
SIZE, THE GOLIATH'S BITE IS PAINFUL
BUT NOT DANGEROUS TO PEOPLE.**

THESE SPIDERS' BITES CAN CAUSE SICKNESS— AND EVEN DEATH!

- **BRAZILIAN WANDERING SPIDER**
  (considered the most deadly)
- **BLACK WIDOW SPIDER**
- **BROWN WIDOW SPIDER**
- **RED WIDOW SPIDER**
- **BROWN RECLUSE SPIDER**
- **REDBACK SPIDER**
- **FUNNEL WEB SPIDERS**

Around **1.2 million**
people are stung by

SCORPIONS

every year. Some stings can
be fatal, and they kill around
3,200 people per year.

The deadliest scorpion
is thought to be the

DEATH STALKER,

which has very powerful venom.

If a scorpion's pincers are very large, it is less likely to have powerful venom. Small, weak pincers mean that the scorpion needs an extra weapon—strong venom to paralyze prey.

Deadly
in the
Air

barn owl

MANY **OWLS** HAVE SPECIAL WING FEATHERS THAT MUFFLE THE SOUND OF THE AIR RUSHING OVER THEIR WINGS AS THEY FLY. THESE ALLOW THE OWL TO HUNT QUIETLY AND STEALTHILY TO GRAB ITS PREY BY SURPRISE.

64

A BARN OWL SWALLOWS MICE WHOLE AND CAN EAT AROUND 1,000 MICE A YEAR.

A **snowy owl** has super-sharp eyesight and razor-sharp talons. It uses them to catch and eat as many as 1,600 lemmings a year.

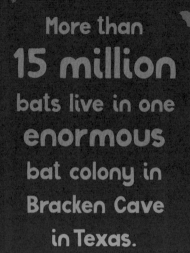

More than **15 million** bats live in one **enormous** bat colony in Bracken Cave in Texas.

Every **sunset** they leave the cave to go out hunting, catching more than **100 tons** of **moths** between them every night.

THE HARPY EAGLE

HAS 5 IN. TALONS—LONGER
THAN A GRIZZLY BEAR'S
CLAWS. IT USES THEM TO
GRAB AND GRIP ITS PREY,
WHICH ARE MOSTLY
MONKEYS AND SLOTHS.

THE **BLACK HERON** SPREADS ITS
WINGS IN A CIRCLE OVER WATER TO
MAKE SMALL FISH THINK THAT THE
WATER THERE IS IN SHADE AND COOL.
AS THE FISH SWIM OVER, THE HERON
PLUNGES ITS SHARP BILL DOWNWARD
TO SNAP UP THE FISH.

harpy eagle

Vampire bats

only eat BLOOD,

which provides

them with all the

food and drink they need.

~

They make a small bite with their
ultra-sharp teeth and then lap up the
blood that flows out.

Vampire bats
mostly bite birds, cows,
and other farm animals,
but will sometimes
bite humans!

71

Bald eagles
are mighty birds of prey.

They can soar high in the air for hours, using their sharp vision to hunt for prey.

bald eagle

Pairs build huge nests out of tree branches for their young. The biggest was 9.5 ft. wide and weighed around 2 tons!

Eagles hunt a wide range of creatures with their **razor-sharp talons**, including hares, rabbits, small deer, grouse, and fish. Golden eagles sometimes **drag** or **push** mountain goats off cliffs to kill them!

A
PIPISTRELLE
BAT

is only 1.5 in. long and weighs
0.3 oz. or less, but it is a

FEROCIOUS
HUNTER.

Flying at high speed, it
can consume 3,000 insects
in a single night.

Most bats eat insects, but the **greater bulldog bat** prefers fish! It flies just above water and sends out sound signals that bounce off any fish near the surface. Once spotted, the bat will grip a fish with its large, clawed feet.

THE **TARANTULA HAWK** IS ACTUALLY A TYPE OF WASP. IT USES ITS POWERFUL STING TO PARALYZE A FEARSOME TARANTULA SPIDER AND THEN DRAGS THE SPIDER TO ITS BURROW.

A ROBBER FLY

HAS SUCH FAST
REACTIONS THAT
IT CAN CATCH A
GRASSHOPPER IN
MIDAIR. IT GRABS
PREY WITH STRONG,
BRISTLY LEGS.

A **KESTREL**
can hover high above
the ground and use
its keen eyesight
to spot a
BEETLE
165 ft. away.
Its favorite food is
the field vole, and
sometimes it also
hunts mice and
small birds.

The **HOODED PITOHUI** bird is **highly poisonous**. It contains the same **dangerous toxins** that are found in lethal **poison dart frogs**. If a predator eats the bird, it's unlikely to survive.

The PARADISE TREE SNAKE glides from TREE to TREE in Southeast Asia by holding its body in an S-shape. It roams through forests, hunting geckos, bats, and frogs.

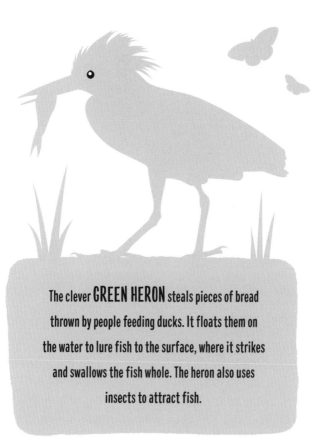

The clever **GREEN HERON** steals pieces of bread thrown by people feeding ducks. It floats them on the water to lure fish to the surface, where it strikes and swallows the fish whole. The heron also uses insects to attract fish.

Deadly
in the
Water

THESE ARE THE THREE KINDS OF SHARKS THAT ARE MOST LIKELY TO ATTACK HUMANS:

1. Great white sharks
2. Bull sharks
3. Tiger sharks

But shark attacks are very rare, and most kinds of sharks don't attack people.

great white shark

The **archerfish** uses its mouth as a **water pistol**. It fires bullets of water to **knock** insects off plants and into the water, where it can **gobble them up**.

The **FROGFISH** is one of
the **fastest hunters** of
all creatures. It can lunge and capture
its prey (usually smaller fish)
in just **0.006 seconds!**

Crocodiles are some of the world's most dangerous predators. They spend time on land but are happiest in the water, where they can swim at speeds of up to 19 mph and hold their breath underwater for up to an hour.

Leopard
～ seals ～

eat a wide variety of food,
from tiny, shrimp-like krill
up to crabs, fish, squid,
and other seals.

Their favorite prey
seems to be PENGUINS.
An adult leopard seal can
eat six penguins a day!

Imagine a river fish almost as deadly as a great white shark! In Africa,

goliath tiger fish

swim in the Congo River. They have 32 large,

dagger-like teeth,

and will even take on crocodiles in a fight!

The **PUFFER FISH** can **inflate** itself so that all its **SPINES** stick out, making it look like a comical **spiky balloon.**

The **venom** that coats the **spines** is **no laughing matter** though – it is powerful enough to **kill** a person.

POLAR BEARS
ARE FIERCE MARINE PREDATORS.

They often lie in wait by seal
breathing holes.

POLAR BEARS ARE SO STRONG
THEY CAN HAUL A SEAL WEIGHING
175 LB. OUT OF THE WATER.

ALTHOUGH THEY ARE
STRONG, FIERCE, AND EXCELLENT
SWIMMERS, ONLY TWO OUT
OF EVERY HUNDRED POLAR BEAR
HUNTS END IN SUCCESS.

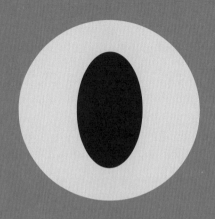

TO SEE THROUGH THE GLOOMY OCEAN DEPTHS,
THE EYES OF THE **COLOSSAL SQUID** ARE
BIGGER THAN A BASKETBALL. THE CREATURE GROWS
TO 43 FT. LONG AND USES ITS LONG TENTACLES
COVERED IN HOOKS AND SUCKERS TO SNARE FISH
AND SMALLER SQUID.

Before it goes hunting, a

SWORDFISH

can pump extra blood to its
eyes to heat them up.

This means they operate faster and see
fast-moving flashes of light such as sea
creatures the swordfish wants to eat.

A LION'S MANE JELLYFISH

can grow up to **1,200 tentacles**, each with stings that can stun their prey.

Their longest tentacles grow to 118 ft. in length—longer than a basketball court.

A BLUE-RINGED OCTOPUS

is small and colorful but deadly.
As it bites, its small, sharp beak injects
poison that is strong
enough to kill a person.

The
geographic cone snail,
which lives in the sea, contains
deadly venom,
that it injects with a long,
needle-like tooth.

It preys on worms
and other snails but
has been known
to kill people.

An **ELECTRIC EEL**
can give off an
electric
shock
of 600 volts.
It uses these
shocks to
stun its prey
—mostly small fish,
lizards, and frogs.

It can also be
dangerous
to people.

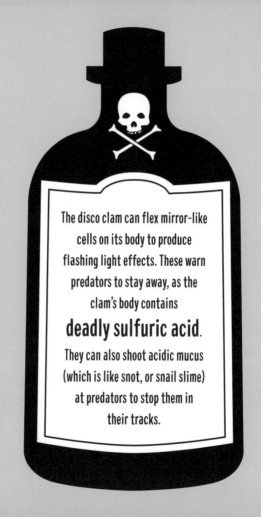

The disco clam can flex mirror-like cells on its body to produce flashing light effects. These warn predators to stay away, as the clam's body contains

deadly sulfuric acid.

They can also shoot acidic mucus (which is like snot, or snail slime) at predators to stop them in their tracks.

Bacteria inside a **web burrfish** create a poison that is 40 times more powerful than **cyanide poison.** Any creature taking a bite out of a burrfish is unlikely to last long!

Nile crocodiles mostly feed on fish but sometimes **LUNGE** out of the water to **GRAB** zebras, wildebeests and young hippos at water holes or rivers. These African crocodiles can eat up to a fifth of their body weight in a single meal.

GUSTAVE,

A GIANT NILE CROCODILE SPOTTED IN THE RUZIZI RIVER AND LAKE TANGANYIKA, IS BELIEVED TO HAVE MADE MORE THAN 300 ATTACKS ON HUMANS.

THIS **KILLER CROC** WAS LAST SEEN IN 2015.

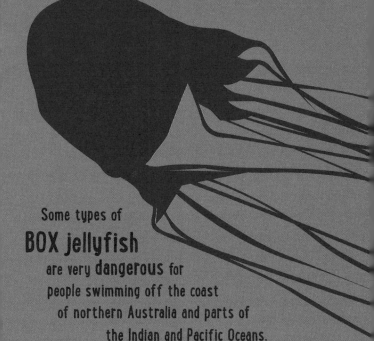

Some types of
BOX jellyfish
are very **dangerous** for
people swimming off the coast
of northern Australia and parts of
the Indian and Pacific Oceans.

Their long, stinging tentacles contain super-powerful
venom that can **kill**. They are thought to be the
most venomous animals in the world.

DEEP SEA **ANGLERFISH**
HAVE A ROD THAT STICKS
OUT FROM THEIR BODIES
TO ABOVE THEIR HUGE
MOUTHS. ON THE END
IS A BLOB THAT
GLOWS IN THE DARK.

THE ANGLERFISH USES
THIS AS A LURE TO ENTICE
OTHER CREATURES TO COME
CLOSE—SO THAT IT CAN
GOBBLE THEM UP.

～ SHARKS ～

are constantly growing new teeth
to replace old ones. Some sharks go
through an incredible 35,000 teeth
during their lifetime.

A BULL SHARK
can detect sounds from
a school of fish over
a mile away.

HAMMERHEAD SHARKS sometimes use their strangely shaped **wide** heads to pin a stingray to the sea floor before they eat it!

The **ALLIGATOR SNAPPING TURTLE**

has powerful jaws that
could easily bite through
a broom handle or
snip your fingers off!

The turtle has a thin red lump growing out of its tongue that looks like a worm.

The turtle sits motionless in water, opens its mouth wide, and waits for fish to be attracted to the red lure and swim right up to its mouth.

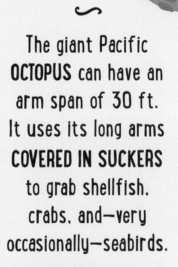

The giant Pacific
OCTOPUS can have an
arm span of 30 ft.
It uses its long arms
COVERED IN SUCKERS
to grab shellfish,
crabs, and—very
occasionally—seabirds.

A sperm whale may dive down 6,500 ft. to chase its favorite food, **GIANT SQUID**, and one was recorded at a depth of over 9,800 ft. The largest sperm whales can weigh more than 55 tons!

YELLOW SADDLE GOATFISH work together to chase and corner other fish to eat.

LIONFISH have 18 venomous spines sticking out of their bodies. They can eat a lot of fish in a day —a lionfish's stomach can expand up to 30 times its normal size!

lionfish

GREAT WHITE SHARKS can swim at speeds up to 35 mph and can detect the faint scent of blood or prey up to 1.300 ft. away. They could smell a drop of blood in a swimming pool full of water.

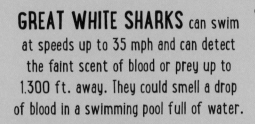

The shark's mouth contains **300 teeth**, each of which have **jagged** surfaces, a little like a saw blade.

A great white shark's BITE is fearsomely strong. It can tear away 33 lb. of meat in one go.

Humpback whales sometimes work together to hunt their prey. They blow lots of

AIR BUBBLES,

which form a sort of net around a school of fish, herding them all together before the whales feast hungrily on them.

AN ADULT
HUMPBACK
WHALE MAY
EAT 3,000 LB.
OF FOOD
A DAY!

The largest ever shark was called

MEGALODON.

It lived between 2.6 and 20 million years ago and measured up to 10 ft. long. That's more than three times the length of a great white shark!

MEGALODON'S
~ MOUTH ~

was around 60 ft. wide
and contained 270 triangular teeth.
Some of these teeth were
7 in. long, giving it tremendous
biting power.

RED-BELLIED PIRANHAS

make barking sounds when they hunt.

Their powerful jaws and super-sharp
teeth shear the fins off larger fish
and can strip a creature's flesh
off its bones quickly.

123

Despite its common name of

KILLER WHALE,

the orca is the largest kind of

DOLPHIN.

It HUNTS a wide range of creatures, including SEALS and SHARKS.

Some orcas grab seabirds resting on the water, or surf waves onto the shore to snatch seals that are lying on a beach.

A large male orca can eat over 440 lb. of food a day!

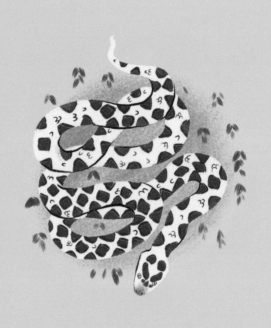

Deadly
Record
Breakers

The deadliest creatures to humans are not sharks, tigers, or snakes, but

MOSQUITOES.

According to the World Health Organization, mosquitoes kill around 600,000 people a year by spreading a deadly disease called malaria.

THE BULLDOG ANT

is the most **dangerous** ant in the world. It lives in Australia, is very **aggressive**, and its venomous bite **can kill.**

Found only on five
islands in Indonesia,

DEADLY

KOMODO DRAGONS are the
biggest lizards on Earth.

They can reach
10 ft. long and weigh
over 285 lb.

131

ᔕ The green ᔕ
ANACONDA

is the world's heaviest snake. Some grow to more than 25 or 30 ft. long and weigh 550 lb.— more than three adult humans.

An adult anaconda can open its mouth so **wide** that it can swallow a wild pig, a deer, or even a jaguar whole!

The largest four-legged hunter on Earth today is the **polar bear**, weighing up to 1,300 lb.

Standing on its hind legs, a polar bear can rear up **11.5 ft. tall**—twice the height of an adult human!

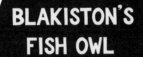

BLAKISTON'S FISH OWL IS THE WORLD'S LARGEST OWL, WITH A WINGSPAN OF UP TO 6 FT. IT PREYS MOSTLY ON FISH BUT ALSO EATS BIRDS AND SOMETIMES BATS.

Many thousands of years ago,
a meat-eating lizard called

MEGALANIA

hunted prehistoric creatures such as turtles
and kangaroos. Megalania was the biggest
lizard ever and weighed up to
1,300 lb.—the same as a big polar bear!

Reaching more than 16 ft. in length, the king cobra is the **LARGEST VENOMOUS** snake in the world. One king cobra can inject enough venom to kill an elephant.

Male

SIBERIAN TIGERS

are some of the most
fearsome predators
in the world. They are the
largest big cats, growing up
to 11 ft. long and 660 lb.
in weight.

The saw-scaled viper kills around 4,000-5,000 people every year—

more than any other snake. This is partly because it lives in areas where there are lots of people.

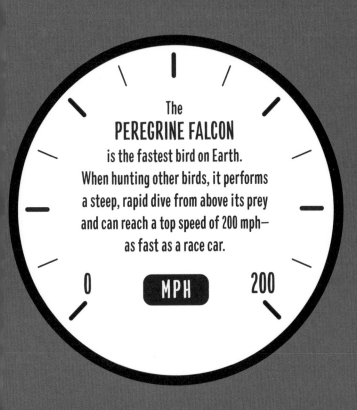

The
PEREGRINE FALCON
is the fastest bird on Earth.
When hunting other birds, it performs
a steep, rapid dive from above its prey
and can reach a top speed of 200 mph—
as fast as a race car.

0   MPH   200

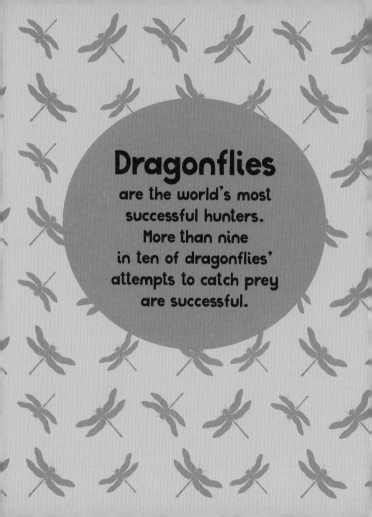

Dragonflies

are the world's most successful hunters. More than nine in ten of dragonflies' attempts to catch prey are successful.

The **SALTWATER CROCODILE** has the **strongest bite** of all animals alive today. Scientists have measured it as 25 times more powerful than a human bite.

∽ CHEETAHS ∽

are the fastest big cats—and the
fastest land animals in the world.
They can sprint from a standstill to
45 mph in just two seconds and
reach a top speed of over 55 mph.